DINOSAUR SCIENCE

ARE CHICKENS REALLY DINOSAURS?

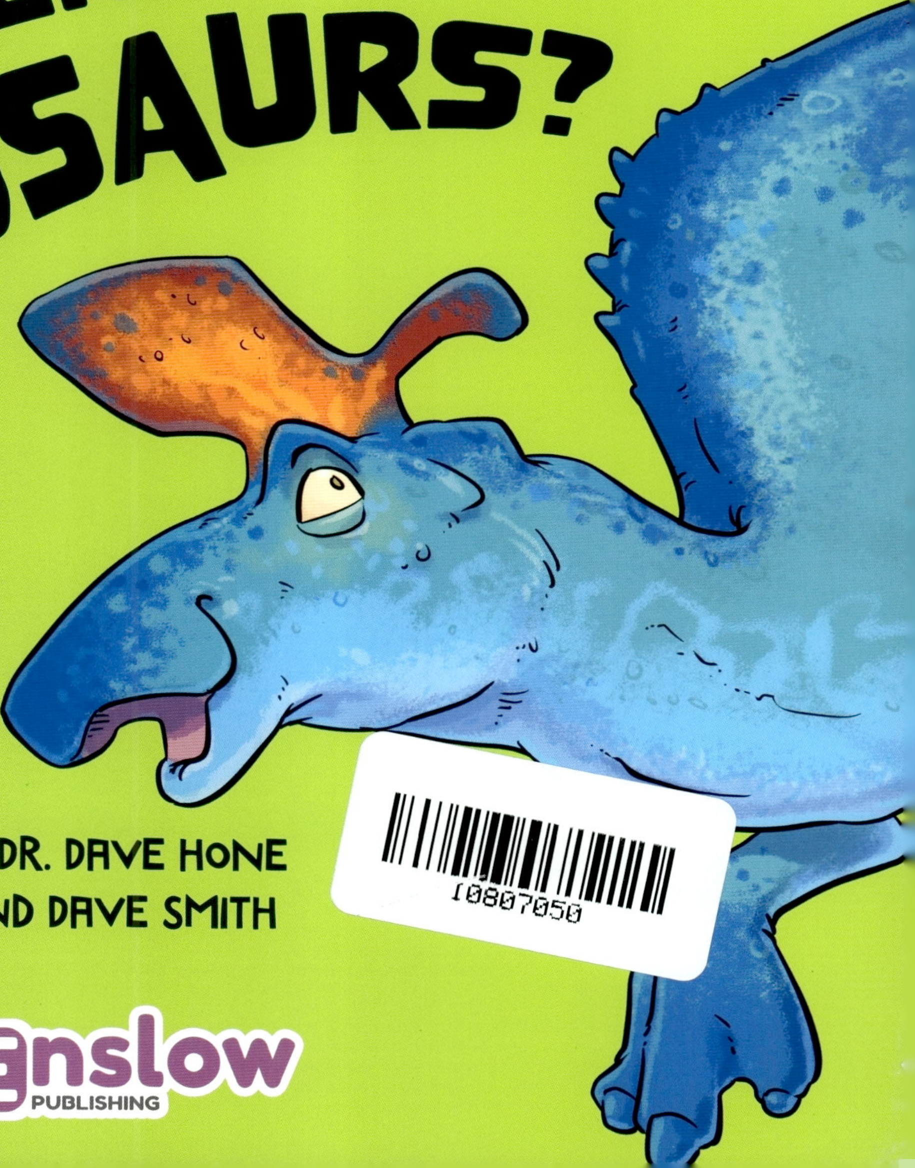

BY DR. DAVE HONE AND DAVE SMITH

Enslow PUBLISHING

Published in 2026 by Enslow Publishing, LLC
2544 Clinton Street
Buffalo, NY 14224

First published in Great Britain in 2023 by Wayland

Editors: Christina Webb and Elise Short
Design: Emma DeBanks

Printed in China

CPSIA compliance information: Batch #QW26ENS: For further information contact Enslow Publishing LLC, New York, New York at 1-800-398-2504.

Please visit our website, www.enslowpublishing.com. For a free color catalog of all our high-quality books, call toll free 1-800-398-2504 or fax 1-877-980-4454.

Cataloging-in-Publication Data
Names: Hone, David (Paleontologist), author. | Smith, Dave, illustrator.
Title: Are chickens really dinosaurs? / by Dr. Dave Hone, illustrated by Dave Smith.
Description: Buffalo, NY : Enslow Publishing, 2026. | Series: Dinosaur science | Includes glossary and index.
Identifiers: ISBN 9781978547254 (pbk.) | ISBN 9781978547261 (library bound) | ISBN 9781978547278 (ebook)
Subjects: LCSH: Dinosaurs--Juvenile literature. | Dinosaurs--Anatomy--Juvenile literature. | Extinct reptiles--Juvenile literature. | Paleontology--Juvenile literature.
Classification: LCC QE862.D5 H66 2026 | DDC 567.9--dc23

CONTENTS

EVERYTHING IS CONNECTED

Every living thing on Earth is related to each other, even if it's from a VERY long time ago. Scientists try to piece together how closely different groups of animals, known as species (see page 10), are related to each other based on their similarities and differences.

Near or Far?

We can work out when animals are closely related to one another by looking at features that they share. For example, all sauropod dinosaurs have small heads on the end of long necks and simple teeth, and they walk on all fours. We use these features to group them together. We can also notice that they are different to the meat-eating theropods that have sharp claws and walk on two legs.

Here are some examples of different theropod dinosaurs and changes over time.

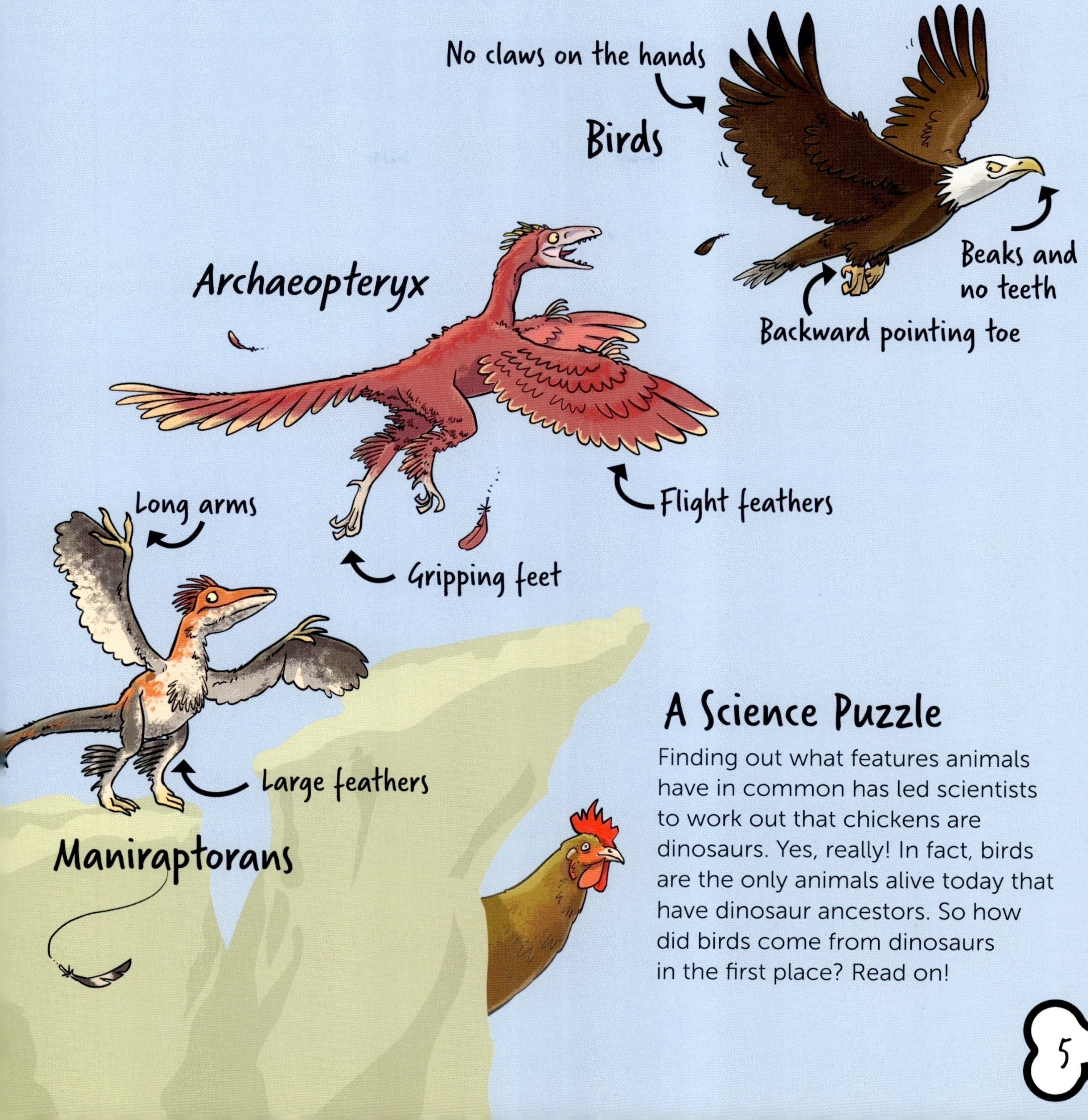

A Science Puzzle

Finding out what features animals have in common has led scientists to work out that chickens are dinosaurs. Yes, really! In fact, birds are the only animals alive today that have dinosaur ancestors. So how did birds come from dinosaurs in the first place? Read on!

EVOLUTION

Just like you're not exactly the same as members of your family, or not every duck on the local pond is identical, not every member of a species is exactly the same. You can pick out differences in size, color, or other features.

Change Over Time

The process of change in living things over time is called evolution. For example, if a new fast predator appears, only the fastest herbivores with the longest legs will survive, as they are more likely to escape the predator. As they are long-legged, their babies will likely have longer legs too. Add up enough changes that improve survival over time, and the later animals might even be different enough to the earlier ones to be called a new species altogether!

Evolution Explains Everything

Many different factors can cause species to evolve and change. They could be changes to where animals live; a place gets hotter or wetter. This can then affect the plants living there: plant leaves get tougher. Or animals change to have better camouflage or hearing so that they don't get eaten by predators. All these things can then affect and change species too. These changes are called adaptations.

DEEP TIME

As it can take thousands of years for changes to build up, it's normally very hard to see evolution happening in one lifetime. This is why fossils, the preserved remains of living things, are the key to helping us look back over millions of years to see how things changed, and try to work out how and why.

Tracking Tyrannosaurs

We can look at different species of tyrannosaur over 100 million years, from the earliest ones to the famous *Tyrannosaurus rex*.

Guanlong wucaii
Late Jurassic Period,
163–158 million years ago

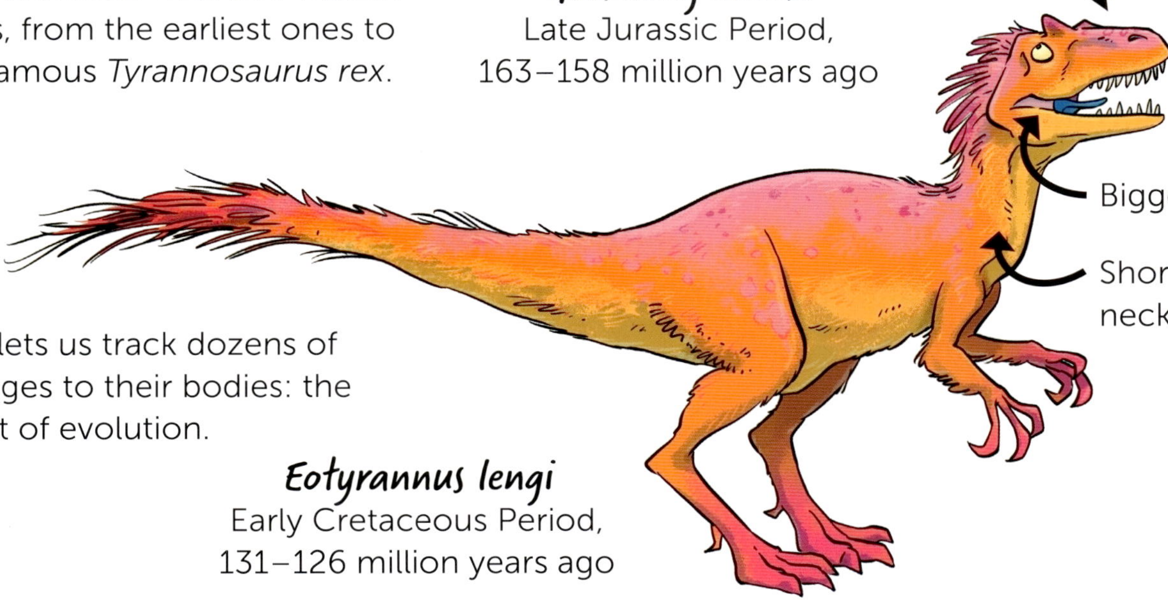

This lets us track dozens of changes to their bodies: the result of evolution.

Eotyrannus lengi
Early Cretaceous Period,
131–126 million years ago

By comparing *Guanlong wucaii*, *Eotyrannus lengi*, and *Tyrannosaurus rex*, we notice that their bodies have changed in many different ways.

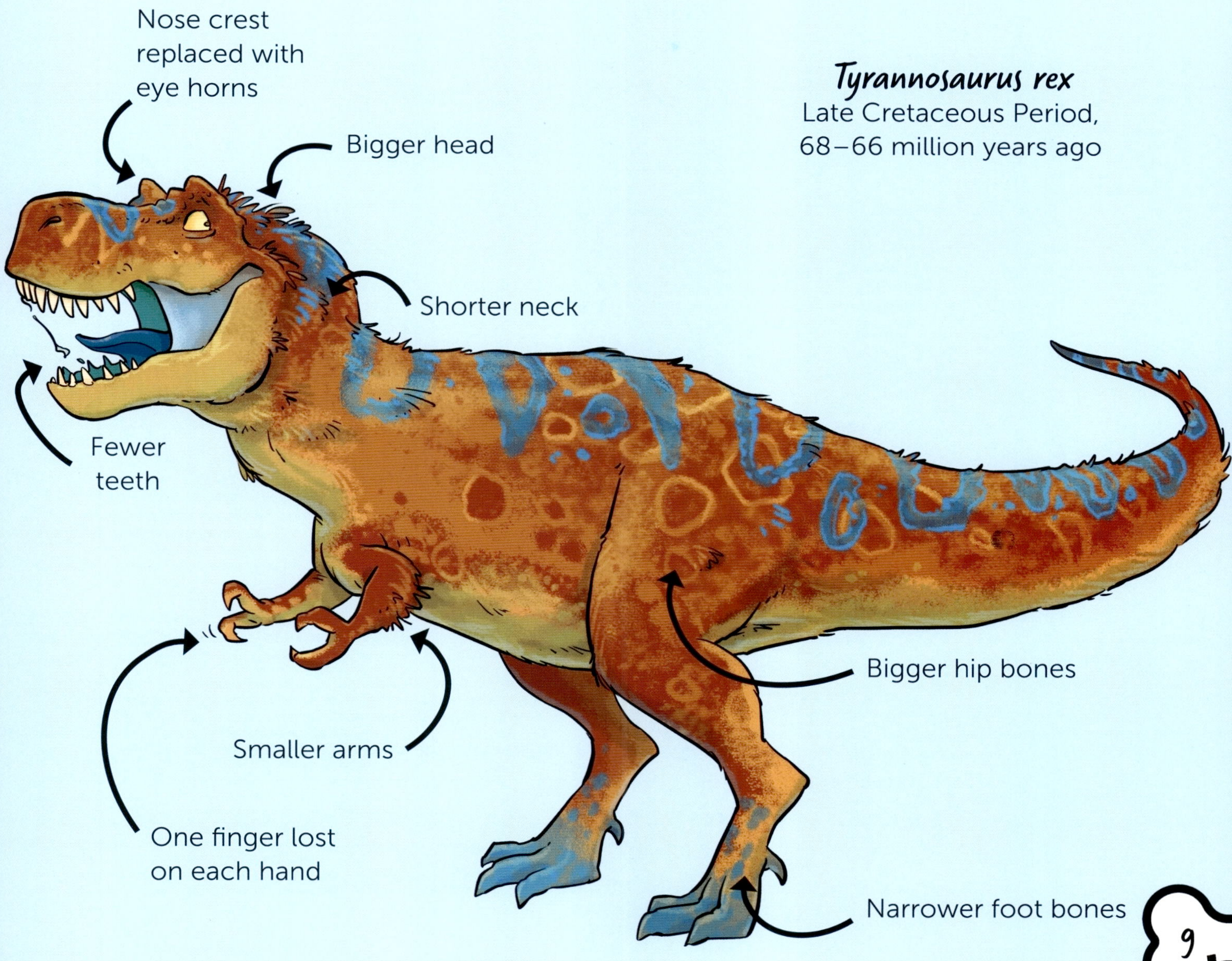

FAMILY TREES

Through looking at features that animals (or plants and other living things) have in common, scientists can piece together the family trees of lots of species.

Same But Different

These three birds are ducks that belong on the duck branch of the bird family tree. But if you look closely you'll see differences: the color of their feathers or the shape of their beak. These differences set them apart enough that they are on their own small branches of the family tree. They are their own species. We can do the same with dinosaurs.

How old?

We can work out how old fossils are from the rocks in which they are found – older rocks sit at the bottom, while younger ones are on top. This allows paleontologists (scientists who study fossils) to put dates on group family trees and trace when a species appeared.

AWESOME ARCHOSAURS

By piecing together dinosaur family trees, scientists have worked out that dinosaurs appeared at the end of the Middle Triassic Period. They came from a group called archosaurs, a name that means "ruling reptiles" as they were the main animals on land for nearly 200 million years. Through evolution, some of these reptiles produced the dinosaurs and some of those became birds.

Everyone's Grandparents

Archosaurs include the flying pterosaurs, crocodiles, and various other animals that went extinct when the dinosaurs took over.

Onward and Upward

Archosaurs were more active and faster than the other reptiles around them and the lizards we know today. This was because they stood up off the ground with their legs under their body, unlike lizards who lie with their bellies close to the ground and their legs sticking out to the side.

DIVERSITY OF DINOSAURS

A lot of the early dinosaurs looked similar because they hadn't had time to evolve in different ways. They were all about 3 feet tall (1 m, or coming up to the waist of the average adult man) and all of them were meat-eaters who walked on their back legs.

Evolution + Time = Diversity

Over tens of millions of years dinosaurs changed into all kinds of different-looking animals and new species. They came in all shapes and sizes with all sorts of weapons, armor, teeth, tails, and displays. There existed everything from the plated *Stegosaurus* to the long-legged *Ornithomimus*, the truly gigantic sauropod *Patagotitan* to the tiny, feathered ant-eating *Linhenykus*. But which dinosaur group did birds evolve from?

DID YOU KNOW?

For the last ten years, paleontologists have named nearly one new dinosaur every week! There are now more than 1,500 known dinosaur species.

THE MYSTERY OF THE EVOLUTION OF BIRDS

Sometimes tracing back the evolution of some species is a puzzle. Where birds came from was a mystery to scientists for a long time. It was hard to work out what animals they might be related to because birds have so many special features (such as beaks and feathers) that they don't share with other groups of animals.

Feathery Stars

Birds are the only animal group that is alive today to have feathers, but they also have scales on their feet like reptiles, and are warm all the time like mammals. The question was, were they weird mammals, weird reptiles, or something else?

First Fossils

Early on in the study of their origins, not many bird fossils had been discovered. And the fossils that were found showed that ancient birds looked just like modern birds, so they didn't give scientists any clues about what other animals birds may have evolved from. It was still a mystery.

THE FIRST BIRD

In 1861 a German scientist discovered a fossil feather from the Jurassic Period – there must have been a bird that lived alongside dinosaurs!

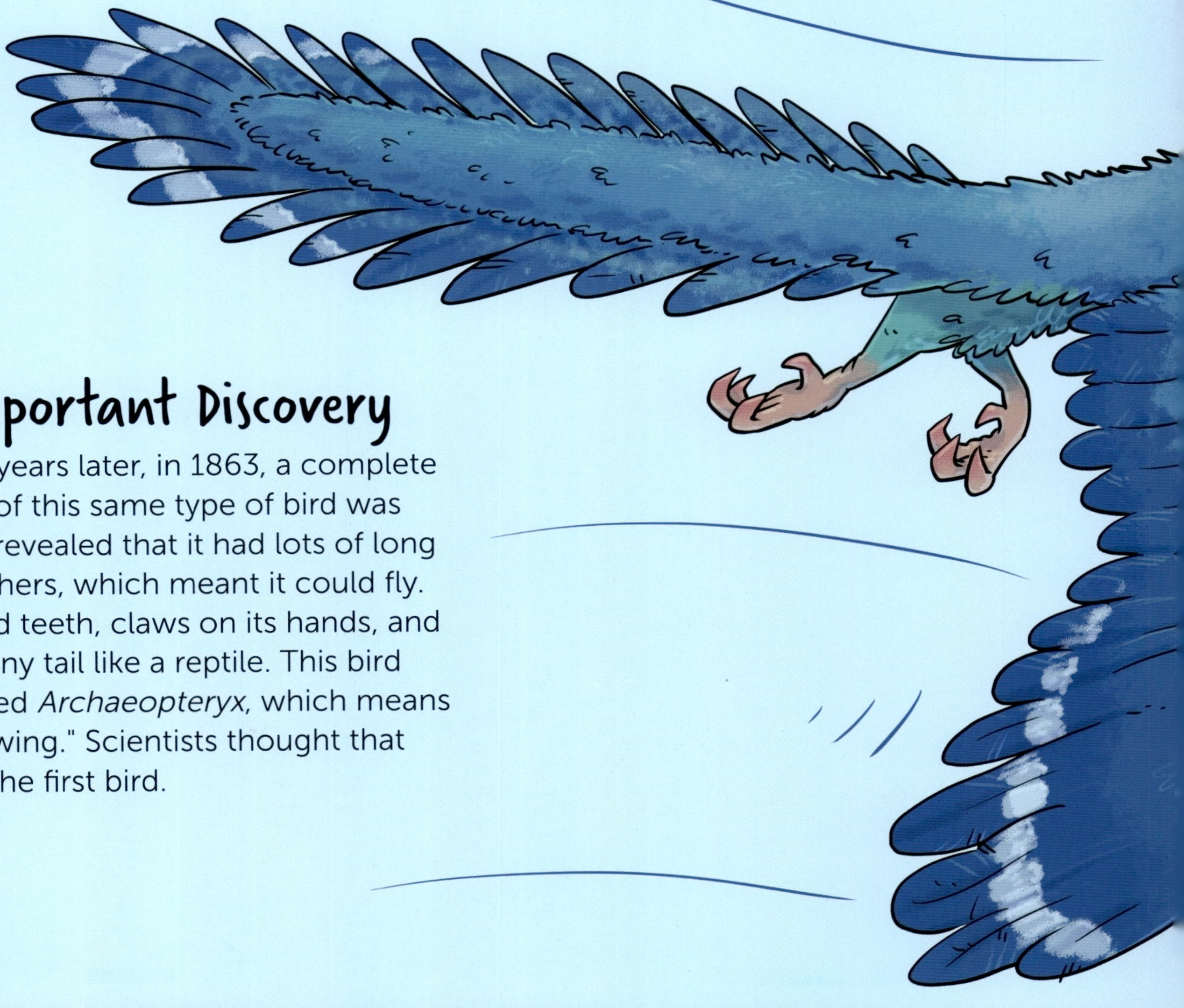

An Important Discovery

Just two years later, in 1863, a complete skeleton of this same type of bird was found. It revealed that it had lots of long wing feathers, which meant it could fly. It also had teeth, claws on its hands, and a long bony tail like a reptile. This bird was named *Archaeopteryx*, which means "ancient wing." Scientists thought that this was the first bird.

An Answer At Last?

The *Archaeopteryx* fossil helped to prove two things: that birds had been around since at least the time of the dinosaurs and that they were part of the reptile family tree because of their types of teeth, claw, and tail. But which group of reptiles did the birds come from? Let's have a look at what features birds had in common with other animals.

DID YOU KNOW?

We have now found a dozen different fossils of Archaeopteryx. Some scientists think that they could actually belong to more than one species of Archaeopteryx.

FEATHERS EVERYWHERE

For decades paleontologists disagreed on what type of reptile birds came from. Some thought they came from small dinosaurs, others thought they might be related to early crocodiles.

Fluffy Dinosaurs!

Finally, in the 1990s scientists discovered *Sinosauropteryx* in China. It was a small carnivorous dinosaur that was covered in feathers. Some scientists think it evolved feathers in order to keep warm. These were simple feathers like those you find on baby birds. So *Sinosauropteryx* would not have been able to fly.

Sinosauropteryx

DID YOU KNOW?

Recent studies on the feathers of *Sinosauropteryx* have revealed their colors! The dinosaur had an orange body and orange feathers and an orange and white striped tail.

Feathery Dinosaurs Big and Small

Since then, we have found dozens of species of dinosaur of all sizes with feathers – some feathered dinosaurs weighed over 1 ton (0.9 mt)! These findings are important evidence that birds evolved from dinosaurs.

NOT JUST FEATHERS

It is not just feathers that show us birds came from dinosaurs. Now that scientists have lots of fossils to work from, they have found all sorts of features on their skeletons that link birds with theropod dinosaurs.

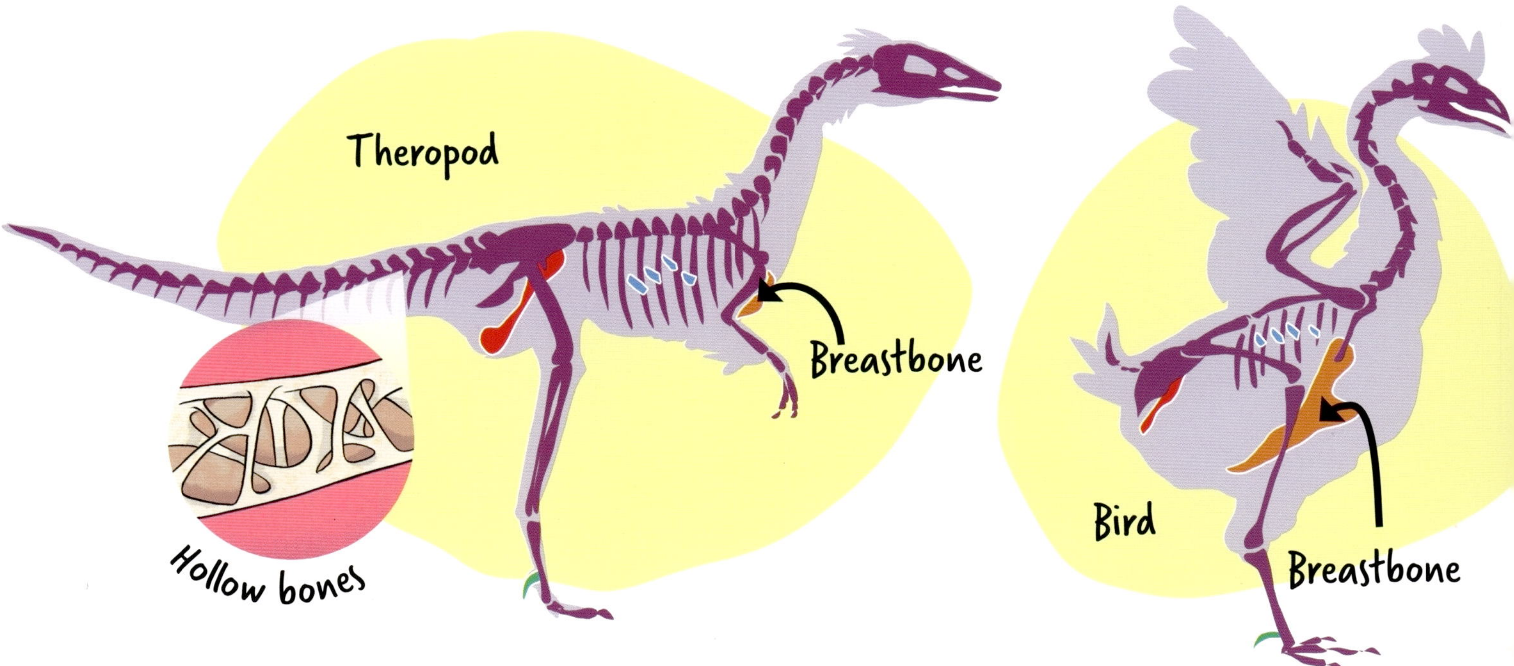

Bone Twins

Both birds and theropods have hollow bones – bones with space for air to flow inside them. Birds also have a huge flat bone on their chest (in orange above) and in later examples of theropods we see this forming too.

Grew Up Together

We now know that birds didn't replace dinosaurs – they lived alongside them for nearly 100 million years! The first birds appeared in the Middle Jurassic Period and were part of the world of dinosaurs from then on.

NOT JUST SKELETONS

Most fossils of large animals come in the form of bones and teeth, but fossils of other kinds can exist too – like fossil footprints, eggs, and nests.

Nest and Eggs

We have now unearthed several dinosaur nests with a parent theropod preserved on top of the eggs. Just like many modern birds, the adult sat in the middle of the nest with a ring of eggs around them. The parents' feathers helped cover the eggs and keep them warm at night and cool in the day.

Hot-bodied

We also now think that many dinosaurs, like birds, were warm-blooded, meaning that their body produced its own heat. They didn't need to get warmth from the sun like other reptiles do. Usually, only warm animals can grow quickly, and because of growth rings in the bones (just like in trees), we can see that dinosaurs grew fast like mammals and birds and not slowly like reptiles.

OTHER ANCIENT BIRDS

After puzzling scientists for a long time, the evolution from theropod to flying bird is now one of the best understood changes in the study of evolution.

More Dinosaur than Bird

Thousands of fossils have now been found that help show the evolution from non-flying theropod dinosaurs into the first birds like *Archaeopteryx*. We also know about the changes that came after *Archaeopteryx*. After all, even though animals like this could fly, they were still more like dinosaurs than birds at this point.

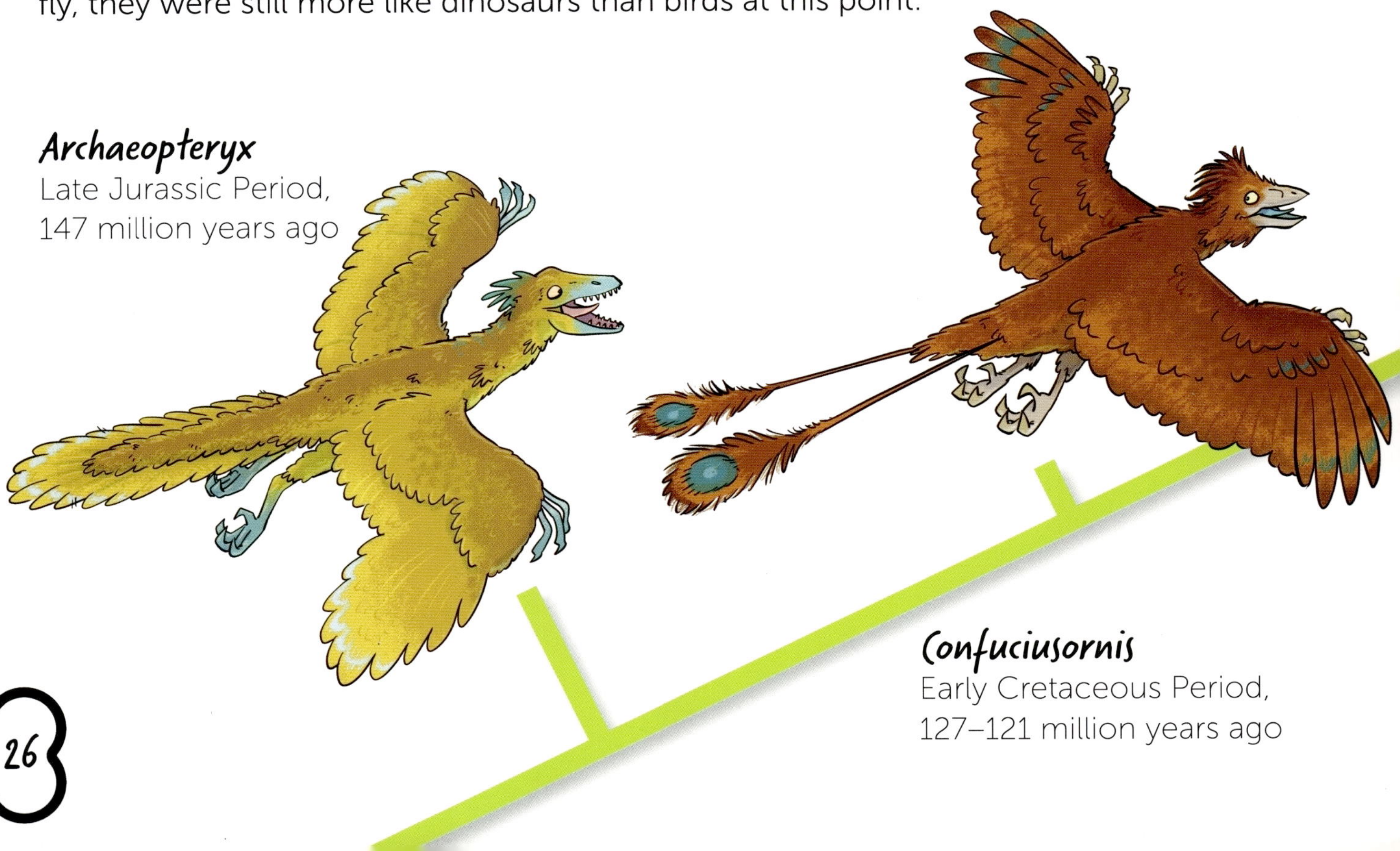

Archaeopteryx
Late Jurassic Period,
147 million years ago

Confuciusornis
Early Cretaceous Period,
127–121 million years ago

Common gull (*Larus canus*)
Alive now

Ichthyornis
Late Cretaceous Period,
95–83.5 million years ago

More Evolution

Fossils show that even before the extinction of the dinosaurs, birds had already changed a lot. They got bigger, started to have longer feathers and grew a bigger breastbone for bigger flight muscles. Their tails shortened and their first toe turned around so that they could grip on branches better. They also lost their teeth and evolved beaks. So the birds that were alive millions of years ago already looked very similar to birds today.

SO CHICKENS ARE DINOSAURS!

So, chickens really are dinosaurs. They have feathers like some dinosaurs, make nests and sit on their eggs like dinosaurs, have hollow bones like dinosaurs, and have big breastbones like dinosaurs.

All Birds Are Dinosaurs

Of course, it's not just chickens that came from dinosaurs, but all birds – all 10,000 species of them! Everything from ostriches to penguins, hummingbirds to the pigeons in your local park – all of them can trace their ancestors back to a single group of small dinosaurs 165 million years ago. These dinosaurs had enough feathers and new features to fly and be called a bird. And they have come a long way since!

What are you doing here?
I'm one of you! But not all dinosaurs are birds ...

GLOSSARY

Adaptation – a feature on an animal that has changed over time to help keep it alive.

Archosaurs – the scientific name for a group of reptiles that includes dinosaurs, birds, crocodiles, pterosaurs, and more.

Dinosaurs – a group of extinct reptiles that were the dominant land animals from around 225–65 million years ago. Their descendants live on today – birds.

Diversity – a range of different things.

Evolution – the natural process where over time species change in response to their environment.

Extinction – the complete loss of a species or group. All the members have died out.

Fossil – the remains of an ancient animal or plant (or remains from their movements, like footprints) that have turned to stone.

Growth ring – a layer of wood, shell, or bone formed in a living thing like a tree trunk during a single period of growth. Scientists can tell how old the bone or wood is by counting the growth rings.

Mammals – a group of animals with four legs and fur. They produce milk for their babies which are usually born from the mother, though a few mammals lay eggs.

Paleontologist – a scientist who studies ancient life. Not just dinosaurs, but also other animals, plants, and ancient environments.

Predator – an animal that hunts, kills, and eats other animals.

Prey – an animal that is hunted and killed for food by another animal.

Reptiles – a group of animals with four legs that usually live on land (though some live in water). They have scaly skin and either lay eggs or give birth to live young.

Species – a set of animals or plants in which the members have similar features to each other and can have babies with each other.

Theropods – a group of meat-eating dinosaurs (though some switched and ate plants) that walked on two legs.

FURTHER INFORMATION

Books

Body Bits: Dead-awesome Dinosaur Body Facts by Paul Mason and Dave Smith (Wayland, 2021)

Dinosaur Infosaurus series by Katie Woolley (Wayland, 2021)

Dino-Sorted series by Sonya Newland and Izzi Howell (Gareth Stevens, 2026)

Websites

Find out about dinosaurs and prehistoric life:
kids.nationalgeographic.com/animals/prehistoric

Watch a video explaining why birds are the only surviving dinosaurs:
www.nhm.ac.uk/discover/why-are-birds-the-only-surviving-dinosaurs.html

Explore the Natural History Museum's directory of dinosaurs:
www.nhm.ac.uk/discover/dino-directory.html

Play games, watch videos and learn about paleontology:
www.amnh.org/explore/ology/paleontology

INDEX